HOW NOT TO HIRE A BAD IMMIGRATION LAWYER

INSIDER SECRETS REVEALED FOR THE FIRST TIME

A PRACTICAL GUIDE TO HIRING THE BEST IMMIGRATION LAWYER

Nasir "Uncle Sammy" Qureshi

TABLE OF CONTENTS

PREFACE

"Don't tell me it's impossible"

~ Muhammad Ali, American professional boxer

Consult with an immigration lawyer! But which one? There are so many. Immigration law is complicated. Who can you trust? How do you know which lawyer is good for you and which one not?

The good news is, yes, it is possible to look for and hire a good immigration lawyer.

You will find information in this book that will help you in finding a good immigration lawyer.

Let's begin and sort this out.

Nasir "Uncle Sammy" Qureshi

What This Book Is Not Designed to Do, My Disclosure & My Disclaimer

This book is not to give you any "legal advice". I cannot give you legal advice because I am not an attorney. The author did not provide any legal advice or interpretation of any law in this book.

This book is not an attempt to seek any immigration clients. The author does not recommend any immigration lawyer or law firm in this book. This book is not an advertisement for immigration law services. This book is for informational, educational, and entertainment purposes only.

I do not guarantee an outcome that you may or may not get by reading this book. I as an author have made all attempts in my due diligence to verify the information provided in this book. The author or the publisher of this book does not assume any responsibilities for errors, omissions, or contrary interpretations on the subject matter stated herein.

Please consult with a competent immigration lawyer before taking any action on your immigration case.

My Qualifications to Write This Book

I am qualified to write this book because of my freedom of speech. I am an immigrant and have gone through an immigration process. I had to hire immigration lawyers. Like anyone else these days, people write reviews, opinions, experiences about businesses. This is my own personal experience, and I am entitled to it.

Not only I have personal experience as a consumer of immigration law. But I also have experience as a senior immigration paralegal with full academic education as a paralegal. I have twelve years of experience as an immigration paralegal working with top immigration law firms in the nation. So I bring an insider experience revealing it for the first time in this book.

Some of the information in this book you will find it to be controversial. Some information you wouldn't be able to find it elsewhere or would not hear anywhere else. Some of the information you would even find it hard to believe. But some things are not meant to talk about and that's why many immigration lawyers will not tell you. But you will find it here.

CHAPTER ONE

INTRODUCTION

"Everywhere immigrants have enriched and strengthened the fabric of American Life" ~ John F. Kennedy

We always hear especially from lawyers that we should consult with an attorney. True, and I agree! But the big question is which attorney should we consult with? Does the attorney have qualifications? Does the lawyer have the experience, and the knowledge to handle your immigration case? Does the attorney know what he or she is talking about? Is he or she a competent immigration attorney? If so, can we put our hard-earned dollars into his or her hands?

This is the dilemma everyone faces when they are looking to hire an immigration attorney.

Being a lawyer doesn't mean that he or she practices immigration law. To practice immigration law, it requires specialized knowledge that not every lawyer has. Not every immigration lawyer has the required experience to handle your case.

This book will help you to solve this big dilemma. It will guide you to help you make the best decision on how to find and hire a good immigration lawyer and avoid a bad one. Hiring a good immigration lawyer could be a difference in achieving the American dream or not! It is that important of a matter!

This is what happened to me

Right after the catastrophic tragedy of 9/11. Immigrants from countries with "special interest" were required to register in thousands. Many were held in immigration detention centers for an indefinite time. Many were placed in immigration courts to answer.

Authorities did what they had to do to protect our homeland. It was understandable. But, this gave a sudden rise to the need for immigration lawyers. Panic between immigrants and especially immigrants from countries with "special interest" grew stronger.

The authorities interviewed me as well. I was all cleared. But that got my attention to the world of immigration law to help. The best way I discovered to help many people was to help them in the court of law and by the law. But there was a problem. I was not a lawyer. I couldn't help them. I couldn't represent them.

I couldn't go to a law school and become a lawyer right away. It takes many years to become one. So I turned to the law libraries to study the immigration law, to dig deep. To make myself familiarized with the immigration law.

That gave me an interest in becoming an immigration paralegal at a law firm. So I decided to become one. But I had no experience. At that time, I was doing odd jobs. I had no professional experience as a paralegal or paralegal education.

So I contacted a friend of mine who was a reputable attorney in town and asked him to help me get a job at a law firm. He sympathized with me and gave me a job at his law firm as a file clerk even though there were no openings at his law firm. To this day, I thank him for helping me jump start my law career.

But my lawyer friend did not practice immigration law. He practiced discrimination law, business law, contract law, state, and federal civil litigation.

I loved the change from doing odd jobs to working in a nice prestigious law firm. It was a professional environment. I was working with brilliant brains. But I wanted to get involved in helping immigrants because I am one. So I kept on looking for openings at the immigration law firms.

Luckily, I found a gentleman who was working as a paralegal at an immigration law firm and was looking for help. I aced my interview and I got my first job as an immigration paralegal at a busy immigration law firm.

There were different immigration lawyers working there. Each one of them had different styles. Thousands of clients. That law firm ran radio ads and did heavy advertisements in the local newspapers. It was a daily adventure and a super busy immigration law firm.

I developed the skills of a competent immigration paralegal. I handled thousands of different types of immigration cases over the years. Before I knew it. I was working with immigration lawyers helping many immigrants and their families. Meanwhile, I started attending a paralegal school on a part-time basis and graduated.

Conflict of Interest of Immigration Lawyers

"Every aspect of the American economy has profited from the contributions of the immigrants."

~ John F. Kennedy, A Nation of Immigrants

In case, if you don't know the definition of "conflict of interest". Please Google it since I tried to keep the legalese in this book to the least.

For any immigration lawyer to suggest which immigration lawyer you should hire could be a conflict of interest for them.

Thus, in my personal opinion, an immigration lawyer is not in the best position to suggest to you who you should hire as your immigration lawyer. Because it would be contrary to their own objectives that they would recommend someone else other than themselves for you to hire.

Let me explain.

Imagine you are asking an immigration lawyer. Who you should hire as your immigration lawyer? It would be like asking a Toyota car salesman which car is the best car in the world. Of course, he would say "Toyota". Further, he would try to give you some reasons. That he is the best, trusting, most reliable, and honest Toyota car salesman in town!

That's why almost every immigration lawyer will suggest to you (indirectly and sometimes directly). That he or she is a good immigration lawyer and the next one may not.

In other words, what we don't want is an opinion of an immigration lawyer who we should hire as our immigration lawyer. We want this decision to hire to be independent and free of the influence of an immigration lawyer.

(By the way. Many immigration lawyers write "Blogs and Forums" online answering questions "for free". So they can drive internet traffic to their own website and get business. Blogs and Forums tend to rank on Google fast. So be mindful of this business tactic of an immigration lawyer). We will discuss this in detail later in this book).

CHAPTER TWO

ABOUT THIS BOOK

"Once I thought to write a history of the immigrants in America. Then, I discovered that the immigrants were American history."

~ Oscar Handline, American Historian

I have written this book by keeping the average person in mind who has no background in immigration law. I do not recommend or promote an immigration lawyer or any immigration law firm in this book.

Instead, I attempted to educate an average reader with the information that could help to find a good immigration lawyer. Once the reader of this book does find a good immigration lawyer. I provided a reader with helpful information on how they should go about consulting with an immigration lawyer. By knowing the right information that they would not know otherwise. Resulting in a well-informed decision when hiring an immigration lawyer.

My style of this book is not to bore you with anonymous and fictitious stories most authors use.

This book is not a "hype book" to get you inspired and pumped you up. If you are looking for inspiration and motivation. This book is not for you.

Once you do complete reading this book. Your confidence level will become higher. Your fears (if any) in hiring a good immigration lawyer will be eliminated.

I can state that you would feel informed, and happy that you purchased this book and you read it.

So let's get right into it.

Why Do We Need This Book?

In my career as an immigration paralegal, I came across thousands of people.

I discovered that most people had no clue what to do when it comes to hiring an immigration lawyer. Most people acted like shooting in a dark room with their eyes closed. This is sad. Unfortunately, many are taken advantage of due to the lack of knowledge.

There will always be a need for immigration lawyers. That's why there are so many immigration lawyers. The United States of America is the best country in the world! For centuries, the U.S. has attracted millions of people. People will continue to migrate to the U.S. despite the politics, changes, and hardships surrounding the immigration law.

An Insider Secret-Immigration Lawyers Will Not Tell You

I am going to surprise you with an insider secret today. I have learned from many immigration attorneys. It's a fact, not a matter of question, and you will never hear this from any immigration attorney.

<u>The secret is that immigration law is not taught in law schools.</u>

That's it. Yes, I said it.

The only thing that is available in law schools about immigration law is an optional elective course for law school students to study. Such courses are short.

Most law school students don't take this short elective course on immigration law, and even if they do, they don't learn much.

Because immigration law is a comprehensive and complicated area of law. It is outlined in the codes of federal regulations in the Immigration Nationality Act (INA). A lawyer has to dedicate for many years to understand and master immigration law.

So how is this important to you?

It is very important for the average person who is hiring an immigration lawyer to know this. It makes the whole world of a difference when it comes to shopping for a good immigration lawyer.

Knowledge and experience of immigration lawyers are different from lawyer to lawyer. If knowledge of an immigration lawyer is limited. He or she may not be able to advise you properly. A lawyer cannot tell you what he or she doesn't know.

Some immigration lawyers may never have handled a case like yours in the past. Therefore, they may not feel confident to handle your case. But they will never tell you that upfront. No immigration lawyer will ever tell you that I don't know immigration law.

This would be up to you to find out whether an immigration lawyer is competent or not.

Yes, I will teach you exactly how you can learn about the immigration lawyer whether he has the experience to handle your case or not.

But this is what happens every day. For a moment, imagine walking into a fancy law firm with beautiful decorations. Big wall certificates, and diplomas hanging on the walls of a lawyer's office. You see volumes of law books in the conference room. A big-screen TV showing the news.

A PowerPoint presentation welcoming you. You have a few magazines about law or news laying around on the table. Many people are sitting in the lobby or fewer. You immediately become impressed with this immigration law firm.

But you don't know the immigration lawyer you are about to see, how much does he or she know about the immigration law?

This is why you need someone to guide you to equip you and prepare you before you go to see an immigration lawyer. This book will help you do that.

Another reason why this book is essential because many people had an open file with an immigration law firm. But they decided to change their immigration law firm and decided to hire another one. There must be a reason for that. Often this costs a person thousands of dollars and many years go wasted.

Some of those issues I will discuss here in this book later on. So you wouldn't have to make those mistakes saving you thousands of dollars and a few years of time.

I decided to write this book for one more reason. Many people when faced with immigration law issues have questions. Should they do a little research themselves or should they fill out forms by themselves?

Should they hire an immigration lawyer or go to a nonprofit organization to get some help?

CHAPTER THREE

FINDING A GOOD IMMIGRATION LAWYER

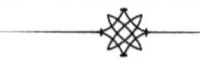

"This is America, a brilliant diversity spread like stars, like a thousand points of a light in a broad and peaceful sky."

~ George H. W. Bush

This is what most immigrants love and most immigration lawyers hate!

Does every lawyer in the United States of America know how to practice immigration Law?

The answer is simple, <u>NO</u>. And that's where the problems begin for an average consumer.

What do most immigrants love and the most immigration lawyers hate? "THE TRUTH".

Ready? Here it is.

One thing that's common between every lawyer is that all lawyers are licensed to practice law. But this doesn't mean that all lawyers do practice immigration law. Or they have the knowledge and qualified experience to do so. Law itself has so many areas of law.

Let me give you a few examples of different areas of law. Family law, divorce law, personal injury law, social security law, disability law, veterans law, state criminal law, federal criminal defense law, federal law, federal civil law, bankruptcy law, discrimination law, business law, contracts, medical malpractice law, legal malpractice law, corporate law, state appellate law, federal appellate law, and tax law are to name few areas. There are so many areas of law and this is not a complete list of all areas of law.

Immigration law is one area among the many. Although immigration law is very comprehensive. Does every lawyer know how to practice immigration law?

The simple answer is <u>NO</u>

Does every immigration lawyer know all about the immigration law?

The answer is No again.

Wait!

Are you telling me that all immigration lawyers don't know all about the immigration law?

Yes, exactly!

A common person who is desperate or is innocent about immigration law facing immigration law questions or issues automatically assumes that the immigration lawyer they are talking to knows all about the immigration law.

Unfortunately, the hard truth is sometimes far away from reality.

By now, you might be thinking, how is that possible?

Great question!

Answer to this question lies in if we briefly understand how a lawyer learns immigration law if immigration law is not taught in law schools?

Here is the answer.

A new lawyer who passed the state bar exam. Now is allowed to practice whatever areas of law they like. New lawyers often are desperate to take any job offers after studying for years. They also have mountains of student debt loans.

In this case, they want to practice immigration law. The first thing a new lawyer would do is land a job at an immigration law firm. Once hired, they will take on some immigration cases, and when they have some questions. They will go to the senior immigration lawyer of the law firm, and there is nothing wrong with that.

New lawyers shadow seniors a few times to the court hearings, citizenship interviews, etc. So they can learn hands-on knowledge. This sometimes puts a great influence on the style of the law practice of a new lawyer.

A senior attorney of the law firm might be the owner of the law firm or might be one of the partners. He or she had worked very hard in the past and made a name for himself or herself. But now they don't care about working that hard anymore on every single case. So they hire newbie lawyers.

Newbies will go through different types of immigration cases. It helps them develop their own styles to practice law. They move on when he or she is ready and has learned enough practical ropes of the profession

Most immigration lawyers have a desire to start their practice. A small percentage remain working for others for the rest of their careers.

This also answers a common question many people have dealing with immigration lawyers. Why do I see a new attorney every time I visit my immigration law firm?

A rookie lawyer hangs around for a while until he or she thinks that they have learned enough and moves on their own.

This makes a lot of people uncomfortable. This gives them the impression that the law firm was there to take their money only and nothing else.

The main attorney of the firm might be good at getting the business in and how to sign up many clients than the rookie one!

This happens a lot with midsized law firms or big law immigration law firms. (Generally, a mid-sized law firm is where the staff is somewhere between ten to twenty people. A big law firm is where the staff is about twenty or more employees).

Once the client is on board. The main attorney passes the file down to the rookie attorney with notes or advice. This is fine to do according to ethics.

I heard many complaints from clients that the lawyer who was working on their case didn't do a good job. Senior attorney blames it on the attorney that is no longer with the firm. By the way, take a note. That a lawyer has a professional responsibility to inform their clients. That another lawyer will handle their case.

Most responsible immigration lawyers do this through a phone call, letter, or email. Unfortunately, many don't!

It puts pressure on a new lawyer when the previous lawyer did not give an update to the new lawyer who is taking over. This puts pressure on the new lawyer. Because he is playing catch-up with files.

Sometimes a client's file doesn't get the attention it deserves. Until a client calls for an update. Many clients don't call till a year or two being busy with other things in their lives. Unfortunately, this happens at many law firms. Many immigration lawyers will never admit to this.

Knowledge of a lawyer depends on the type of cases they have handled. Also, it depends on what law firms they have worked with before. What lawyers they worked with or are working with. The type of immigration cases they take. Because there are different areas within the immigration law.

Some lawyers and law firms take cases that deal with deportation only. Some do family-related immigration cases. Some do employment-related immigration cases. Some lawyers are good at helping people with getting their naturalization and citizenship. Some lawyers focus on waivers. We will discuss this in detail later on.

That's why it is good to know that knowledge of an immigration lawyer to another is not the same. Thus, it is not wise for us to assume that every single immigration lawyer in the nation knows what they are doing. Their knowledge is equal to all other immigration lawyers. They must know immigration law. Because they are a "lawyer". Unfortunately, this is not the case.

Later, I will show you how you can ask a few good questions to a lawyer and get a great insight into their knowledge and experience.

"As an immigrant, I appreciate far, more than the average American, the liberties we have in this country."

~ Gloria Estefan

The Magic Question of "Specialization" in Immigration Law

When many people call immigration law firms. Often they ask if the law firm specializes in immigration law? Even some lawyers use this word "specialized" loosely. But let me explain what specialization means.

There is no "specializing in immigration law". But there is something called a lawyer being a "Board Certified" lawyer.

A "Board Certified" immigration lawyer is a lawyer who has practiced for five years or more in a particular area of law, has taken an optional exam with their state bar, and paid an application fee, and become a "Board Certified" in that specific area of law. That's it.

For example, a lawyer in Texas has to have at least five years of experience, where at least three involve substantial involvement with the specified specialty area and complete the Board-approved Continuing Legal Education (CLE) [educational courses that are mostly completed online on-your-own-pace basis] requirements. That's it. For more details, see:

https://www.tbls.org/Cert/AttyGetStarted.aspx

(Please be mind full that these requirements for becoming a "Board Certified" lawyer may vary from state to state. Kindly, check your state requirements for details).

But is it required for every immigration lawyer who is practicing immigration law to become Board Certified?

The answer is no. They don't have to be. Of course, lawyers know about it. But, unfortunately, the average person doesn't.

It's a little credential if any lawyer wants to get it. They can get it. In fact, most immigration lawyers don't care about this credential and don't pursue it. But, there are immigration lawyers that do get this extra credential.

It doesn't mean that board-certified immigration lawyers are better than those who are not. In fact, I know so many top-notch competent immigration lawyers even former immigration judges who are now practicing immigration law are not Board Certified immigration lawyers.

(Back to the common usage of the word "specialization").

I understand why people use the word "specializing". Because they're so used to hearing this word in the medical industry.

How Can You Find Out Who Should Be Your Next Immigration Lawyer?

Who should be your immigration lawyer? Trust me, your life and your future can depend on it. It is that important if you or you know someone that has some immigration law issues!

Immigration law is a serious business. I take immigration law as a serious matter as most immigrants do. Because I know what immigrants go through in the immigration process!

A good or bad immigration law help can make a difference between achieving the American dream or getting deported. That can depend on experience and the knowledge of the immigration lawyer.

An immigration lawyer can screw up a good case if they don't know what they are doing. This happens a lot throughout the United States of America on a daily basis. (Unfortunately).

One day I was standing in the line at a restaurant waiting for my order. I said hello to a man standing next to me. He was waiting for his food order too. I asked him whether he comes here often and if he likes the food here.

He told me. He is new in town. I asked him where he is from. He said. He is from Iraq. He moved to the U.S. two months ago. He asked me what I do for a living. I told him. I am an immigration paralegal and work in an immigration law firm. He said he was very happy to meet me and shared his story.

He told me that he had no relatives in the U.S. and he didn't know anyone. He was looking for a good lawyer that could help him to file his paperwork with immigration. So he saw an advertisement of a lawyer in a local Newspaper. From the ad, the lawyer looked like. He was very experienced. So I went to see him. He charged me one thousand dollars to do law research in my case to give me some answers. Two weeks later. I got a call from him that he couldn't help me and sent me an invoice saying that he spent a few hours doing law research and the money I paid him is gone.

I didn't know what to do next. Someone told him that he needs an immigration lawyer, not any lawyer. So that person referred him to an immigration lawyer he knew.

He called that immigration lawyer and scheduled a consultation with him. Immigration lawyer charged him $100 for a 15 minutes consultation and advised him that he needs to get married to get his papers straight. There is no other way.

Later, someone informed him that the lawyer he saw, was a car accident lawyer and not an experienced immigration lawyer. He told me that he kept losing money with many lawyers. He doesn't work since he doesn't have an authorization to work in the U.S. He has very limited savings which is about to run out. He has been praying for help. He needs to solve this problem soon or he would be devastated.

I told him that it is true that he needs a lawyer who has good immigration law experience. Who knows what they are doing. One of the best ways to assure that is to go to an immigration law firm who practices immigration law or have a good experience.

So he asked for my help. I scheduled him to see the immigration lawyer I was working with. He visited the immigration lawyer at our law firm and found out. He qualified to get his permanent residency (green card) in the U.S. since he worked as a translator for the U.S. troops in Iraq. The lawyer informed him that he will also get his work permit approximately 3-4 months after filing his paperwork.

This came true after several months. He had his work authorization, a driver's license and a social security number. He started to work as a pharmacy technician. About two years later. He had his permanent residency (a green card) in the U.S. He started going to University of Houston to become a Pharmacist. Today, he is a Pharmacist, married and has one child. He lives in the suburbs of Houston. His whole life changed for good.

Where To Find A Good Immigration Lawyer

When we buy things. We actually make two decisions. One, where we are going to buy it from and from whom. Second, the actual decision of buying. (Sometimes we make several tiny decisions).

Let's look at this human natural phenomenon a little deeper with case studies.

Case study 1:

Imagine, if we want to travel with our family for a family vacation. So the first decision would be where to? For example, if we make a decision that we want to go to Florida for a family vacation (first decision made).

Let's say you are in Dallas, Texas and want to travel to Florida from Dallas. Then, we have to decide. How would you be traveling to Florida? By car or would you be flying and you decided by car (second decision made).

Case study 2: (Continuing the same example)

Now we have to decide where we would get the car rental from and how?

We will consider our resources for getting the best car rental that we would desire. For example, we will look online for deals, recommendations, car rental apps, our memberships, insurance incentives, car rental programs from our jobs and much more. In this example, you decided to go with your online search at www.priceline.com (first decision made for where you would get your car rental from).

Now, you would enter your travel dates, size of the vehicles, check prices and make your selection, add details and make a payment. (Second and final decision made to buy).

Case study 3:

Imagine, you want to go out to watch a movie at the theaters. First,you would decide which movie that you would like to watch (first decision made). Second, which cinema would you like to watch at, and why there? (Second and final decision made to buy).

As you can see that we make at least two decisions before we buy almost anything. First, from where we will buy it. Then, we check and make our second final decision to buy. This is how we are wired as human beings and it's normal.

Most people look for immigration lawyers from the following sources:

1. Referrals from friends, family, and community.

2. Online.

3. Newspaper, TV, radio ads.

4. Lawyers Workshops

For example:

Imagine your sister received a $200,000 lawsuit settlement. Her lawyer was handling her lawsuit for the last three years. She built a good trust and a business relationship with her lawyer. She is happy with her lawyer. She has confidence in her lawyer. She would recommend him to anyone.

You asked her if she knows a good lawyer. She refers you to her lawyer. But her lawyer does not practice immigration law. You don't know that and you don't know how to find that information. This could be a time waster deal for you. In this case, you may end up going to see your sister lawyer and he will tell you. He cannot help you or he may refer you to an immigration lawyer that he knows and trusts or he may not. You may contact and go see the immigration lawyer your sister's lawyer recommended. But again, all this can be very time consuming for you.

In this scenario, the trust factor was there. But not the knowledge and experience factor of the immigration lawyer.

It is too long to put all sources in this book where you can find a good immigration lawyer. Also, your location can be everywhere in the world. So I rather equip you with the right information so wherever you are. You can make a good and informed decision in hiring a good immigration lawyer and avoiding a bad one!

These are very important factors that you should consider when you are finding one.

a. *The trust factor*: Do you know someone that had success using the same immigration lawyer?

b. *Type of immigration law*: There are different categories within the immigration law. Know the category of your immigration case. In other words. You should at least know the nature of your immigration case. You should find out whether the immigration lawyer handles the same type of immigration cases as yours or not.

c. *Experience*: Is the lawyer a new lawyer or has been practicing for some time? How many years the immigration lawyer has been practicing immigration law? (I will discuss this matter in detail later in this book).

d. *Customer service*: How is the customer service of immigration law? Do they care? Do they answer your questions? Do you feel comfortable giving your case to them? Will they answer your questions when needed? (I will discuss this matter in detail later in this book).

e. *Knowledge*: Is the lawyer knowledgeable about the immigration law? And how much? (I will discuss this too in detail later).

f. *Success rate*: We also want to find out generally what is the success rate of the immigration lawyer? And what is the success rate of the "category" of your immigration cases the lawyer has handled so far? There are two different things. The success rate of the lawyer and the success rate of immigration cases.

g. *Location*: This factor may be very important to many. Where is the immigration lawyer located at? Across the city? Different cities or states? Can they work with you through a secured online portal? Some immigration lawyers work in person. Some only work through an online system and never meet a client in person. Location matters!

h. *Payments*: This is an important factor in hiring an immigration lawyer. Can you afford the immigration lawyer? What kind of payment plans does the immigration lawyer offer or not? How much payment does the lawyer need upfront? Full, partial, or monthly payments. What is the down payment, if any? Different immigration lawyers offer different options and charge in a different way. Understand those options. (I will discuss those later in the book).

i. *Work*: It's very important for you to consider how immigration lawyers will work on your case? Some lawyers do all the work by themselves. Some do partial work and their assistants do the rest. Some lawyers supervise only and don't do any work themselves. Sometimes, a senior lawyer supervises a rookie lawyer doing the work.

Consultation With An Immigration Lawyer

Let's begin by discussing the consultation process with an immigration lawyer. Because your business relationship with an immigration lawyer begins with a consultation.

An average consultation with an immigration lawyer lasts for thirty to forty minutes. A quick one goes for five minutes to fifteen minutes on average. If the immigration lawyer is good, it will take them thirty to forty minutes to do a consultation. Generally speaking, an average consultation of five to thirty minutes long is insufficient time to be fair. But the reason they do that is that they don't want to spend talking about one immigration case. They want to give you enough time to get to know you, so you can get to know them, ask a few questions, and let you make the decision. Then, who is next? They have to run their business. Yes, immigration law firms are a business.

Would it be better for you that you are aware of good questions that you can ask the immigration lawyer? Try to make the best usage of your time with the immigration lawyer since that time is alway so short for a consultation.

It would be more effective if you are more equipped with good questions not only about your cases. But also about the immigration lawyer.

It is well known that one who asks the questions, controls the conversation.

So true. Let's begin.

Questions To Ask an Immigration Lawyer that the Others Wouldn't

Kindly keep in mind that these questions are polite, professional, and normal to ask. Don't be afraid to ask these questions to the immigration lawyer. In fact, an immigration lawyer would respect you more that you are not an "average Joe" who he can take an advantage of!

The first thing you want to know is when the lawyer became licensed to practice law. You can find this information from the attorney's profile through the law firm's website. If you want to ask the lawyer, you can use these exact words:

"What year did you become licensed as an attorney?"

The second thing you need to find out is how much experience this lawyer has in immigration law. So you ask:

"What percentage of your law practice do you focus on immigration law?"

Let me explain why this question is SO important. Many immigration lawyers just don't practice immigration law. Ready for another hard truth? Here is the "sticker-shock". Every lawyer's knowledge is limited!

Hold on, are you telling me that every lawyer's knowledge is limited?

Exactly.

Let me explain. Every lawyer we know is human. They have personal and family commitments, and all other things to do just like you and I do. So let's say they have a 8 am - 5 pm schedule, Monday to Friday, or a 7 am - 6 pm schedule, as a normal business day.

Lawyers generally divide their time in three parts on a business day. For easy math, let's say they work nine hours a day. One third of their day will be divided or dedicated to mostly attending court hearings. And speaking of immigration lawyers, most of the immigration hearings such as citizenship interviews, green card interviews, visiting clients in detention centers, court hearings, immigration trials, court filings etc., are dedicated to the first three or four hours early in the morning.

The second or third part of the day, which is about three hours where immigration lawyers normally work on files of existing clients or return phone calls, talk to immigration officials on the phone or do telephonic hearings with different courts nationwide, talk with paralegals and do the law research, etc.

Now, the third part of the day, which is approximately three hours, they see existing clients or new clients to keep the business running.

Having said that, think about this, if a lawyer who practices different areas of the law is what we call a "general practitioner"not just the immigration law will most likely have limited knowledge of immigration law compared to an immigration lawyer who has only been practicing immigration law since the day he or she became a lawyer.

That's simply because that general practitioner lawyer had approximately three hours of his portion of work day divided into many areas of law compared to an immigration lawyer who spent the same portion of his time only in immigration law throughout their career.

But both lawyers are known as immigration lawyers but the difference in their knowledge of immigration law could be significant.

Therefore, this question is very important to ask a lawyer when you are talking to one.

"What percentage of your law practice is dedicated to immigration law?"

So when you ask these two questions,

"When does the lawyer become licensed to practice law?"

and;

"What percentage of your law practice do you focus to immigration law?"

You will get a pretty good idea about the knowledge and experience of that immigration lawyer.

Now, the third question you may want to ask is:

"What area of immigration law do you generally practice the most?"

This is a very important question. Because immigration law is generally divided into three major categories. One is family based. Second, employment-based and third is removal defense, which is also known as deportation defense.

(A little percentage of immigration lawyers have dedicated themselves to another sub-category that deals with waivers.)

Without going into too much detail, the family-based immigration law is when a relative is filing a petition or immigration paperwork for another family member. The employment-based immigration category is a world of its own. But to give you an idea, employment-based immigration law is skillful workers seeking immigration benefits based upon their education, higher professional achievements, research or big companies or corporations sponsoring employees to work for their companies in the U.S. This is a broad category itself like the other categories of immigration law.

The third category is a removal defense or known as deportation, which means an immigrant is facing the deportation process in an immigration court. The American government has placed an individual in immigration court proceedings to deport that person, so now the immigrant is in court defending him or herself about why he or she should not be removed (deported) from the United States. This is when an immigrant facing this crisis hires an immigration lawyer to represent him or her in an immigration court.

There are other areas of immigration law as well like post-removal defense, which is very rare that an immigration lawyer practices this category alone. But generally, immigration law is categorized into three areas: family-based, employment-based and removal defense. There are so many types of waivers within the three mentioned-above categories of immigration law. (Some immigration law firms focus on waivers as a whole. Some focus on certain types of waivers alone).

So let's put all this into perspective. You asked them the question about their law practice, what percentage they have dedicated to immigration law, and they said seventy percent. You then ask:

"What do you primarily focus on?" which means, *"What area of immigration law do you primarily focus on?* Removal defense, employment based, or family based.

Let them answer these questions.

Let's say you are filing a case of a family member (which would be a family-based immigration area of law), they say all they do is employment based immigration law. So it would become clear to you that the lawyer before you might have general knowledge or an idea of family-based immigration law. But their primary focus is on employment based immigration law and family-based is not their strength. Now you can make an educated and informed decision to hire this immigration lawyer or not.

These kinds of questions will make things clear whether a lawyer that you're talking to has the knowledge and experience that you're looking for.

There is one more thing you may want to find out on your own online and may not want to ask the lawyer. Whether they have had some kind of trouble in the past with the state bar and that's very easy and simple to do.

Many of us these days like to do research on the internet. But don't know where to except refer to Google or similar search engines. So let me point it out to you where to look for the right information from the right sources not anywhere on Google.

Find out if the lawyer was in trouble before

"One great error is that we suppose mankind more honest than they are"

~ Alexander Hamilton

How can you find out whether a lawyer you're considering to hire has had some kind of trouble before with the state bar or not? All you have to do is find out from the website of the lawyer which state they're licensed from. Let's say he is licensed from the state of Oklahoma, so you Google the state bar of Oklahoma. Then when you land on the state bar of Oklahoma website, you find a place where you can put a lawyer name and do a search. Then you come across whether that person, that lawyer, has had some kind of issue in the past or not.

At the state bar website, you can even check whether their law license shows "Active", which means that they are allowed to practice and are in good standing with the relative state bar. But if you find some history of trouble or any history of disciplinary actions against the lawyer. You will find indications there most of the time, if any. Then you would know if this lawyer has had some drama in the past.

On a side note, some states in the U.S. a "state bar" do not have authority over lawyers, but a different government office does. For example, if a lawyer is licensed from the State of New York, the New York State Bar of Association doesn't watch over them. The State of New York Supreme Court, Appellate Division Third Judicial Department does. (sounds complicated and weird, right?) But it is what it is. Many immigration lawyers in the U.S. are licensed from the New York state, and once an immigrant wants to hire them or wants some fairness in treatment from them or wants to file a complaint, they are lost.

You can use Google and find contact information of the state bar office or office of the clerk of the Supreme Court of that state and ask them that you are trying to find out information about a lawyer. You would like to know if a lawyer is good to practice law or if they had some trouble in the past with the state, or which website you can go to find this information.

Again, this can be sometimes a tricky thing for some states. But for most states, using Google for the state bar will result in the website of that state bar.

Unauthorized Practice of Law & Immigration Fraud

I assume that you are reading this book because you are looking for a good immigration lawyer. But not sure how to find one.

Keeping an average person in mind, who started looking for an immigration lawyer. It would be fair to shed some light on immigration fraud without diverting too much into this topic.

Unfortunately, fraud does take place when it comes to providing immigration law services.

Many people have set up offices and businesses that are not lawyers and are practicing law. You always want to make sure that the person you are talking with is actually a lawyer and if so, is competent.

Unfortunately, many people think that a form preparer is a lawyer. That happens because many immigrants are new in the country and don't know or they are misled.

Sometimes this happens because of the terminology and the culture difference. For example, in Mexico, *"The Notario Publico"* is actually a licensed lawyer. But a "Notary Public" in the U.S. is not a lawyer and cannot practice law.

Often, many people think that they are dealing with immigration lawyers but they are actually not. They are dealing with a notary public, non-lawyer or a form preparer.

Who Are The Form Preparers?

Form preparers are those who record your answers and assist you by typing information (your answers to the questions) on immigration forms for you (like a typing service). But they cannot give you legal advice <u>only lawyers can</u>.

At the end of each immigration form. There is space in a form prepared to complete their contact information and sign it, if they assisted you. <u>But you must select the form for yourself, and not them</u>.

To find free immigration forms with instructions. Go to www.uscis.gov on the website of the United States Citizenship & Immigration Services. You can also find instructions to the forms there as well.

There is a great article titled *"Avoiding Imigration Fraud-A Guide to Avoiding Fraudulent Immigration Practitioners"* written by a non-profit organization from New York City called Immigration Advocacy NYC USA". This organization operates under the guidance and supervision of immigration attorneys as a non-profit organization. (They look pretty legit. I am not recommending them for anything or for any service nor I have any connection with them. But they wrote a good article on this topic).

Here is the link to this article: https://immigrationadvocacy.com/our-services/avoiding-immigration-fraud/

You can also read more about the common immigration frauds that take place; directly at the website of the United States Citizenship & the Immigration Services with an online tip form.

Here is the link: https://www.uscis.gov/report-fraud

Depends on which state you are currently in. But every state has a committee that oversees and assures that there are no unauthorized practices of law happening within that state. It's called the Unauthorized Practice of Law Committee (UPLC).

If you have any concerns or questions, you can contact UPLC in your state. Just Google:

(UPLC in "name of your state") and you will find their contact information.

Ok, let's get back to "The immigration lawyers" :)

Question of Communication

"How do you communicate with your clients and how often?"

This is an important question you should ask an immigration lawyer in the consultation, which is about communication.

Why?

Most of the problems that arise between immigration lawyers and their clients are as a result of communication. Either lack of communication, a way of communication, or not enough communication.

What happens is that clients are expecting one thing. But the immigration lawyers are doing another. This results in disappointments. When there is a disappointment of any kind, things go south.

For example, clients don't get enough calls back or their lawyer won't return their calls. The stress levels of the client becomes higher. Fear of deportation becomes greater. Anxiety levels rise and problems between an immigration lawyer and clients become bigger.

I understand this to a certain degree. Because when a person hires an immigration lawyer they have a legal problem. That's why they hired an immigration lawyer to begin with. No one hires an immigration lawyer because they have nothing else to do. No one likes to waste their hard earned money.

Immigration law clients have problems. Law firms are not clubs where everyone is having a good, happy time. Immigration law is a serious business for immigrants. The difference between staying in the United States and not. The fear of getting separated from their family or getting deported. The stress levels could be high. Clients are anxious. The only way they can get some relief is by contacting their immigration lawyer.

So when immigration law clients don't get their calls returned as expected. Their feelings get hurt. This leads to disappointment, frustrations, problems, legal grievances and requests for refunds. Then they go seek out another immigration lawyer for a "second opinion".

Guess what, the second immigration lawyer has opened his law firm for business. He or she has expenses, a family to feed. They end up suggesting different ideas to already an angry person. For example, get a refund from the first lawyer or file a grievance with the state bar. They need to get justice. It becomes messy. In my career I have seen it all.

So, it is so CRUCIAL to bring up the communication question and set the expectation to avoid all this drama.

Question number four to ask the immigration lawyer:

How do you communicate with your clients?" or *"What is your communication policy with clients?"*

There are different ways that different law firms communicate and have different policies. So what you are doing by asking this question is not only you are asking an educated question. But you're also setting an expectation between you and the soon to be your immigration lawyer. This can also help you to make a good and comfortable decision to hire this lawyer or not.

Some law firms communicate with their clients thur phone calls and emails. Some law firms only do all emails and no phone calls. Some law firms have a policy to return phone calls within 24-48 business hours. Some law firms have one phone call per client in a week, some in two weeks and others are one call or an email a month. But most don't have any limits. But it is good to know first.

I remember some clients used to call me Sunday morning to get answers or get in touch with the lawyer that I was working with at that time. Some people would call at 9 pm on a weeknight and expect their lawyer to attend to their phone calls and get some answers.

I had heard so many clients complaining about the immigration law firms or lawyers that "you guys never answer our phone calls"!

One time a client complained and she was very upset with our office that you guys never attend her phone calls. I asked her what time you were calling and on which day. She said she called our office when she got off from work because she couldn't use her phone at her work. I asked her when you get off from work. She said at 8 pm. Then, I reminded her that our office closes at 6 pm. That's why you reach our office voicemail at that time.

Some clients think that immigration law firms are like calling a customer service of Amazon or At&t where someone will answer their phone calls and give them answers twenty-four hours a day and seven days a week. Please don't do that!

I am hoping that knowing beforehand about the communication policy of a law firm will cut a lot of frustration that happens between clients and their lawyers for the duration of your immigrtion case.

Life Is Not a Sack of Potatoes!

"America was and is the Immigrant's Dream"

~ Don Delillo, American Essayist and a Novelist

Most people when they have a consultation with an immigration lawyer are having their first experience. They have a mindset of "buying a product" not the mindset of "buying a service". There is a BIG difference and why that is important to you and your immigration law case!

Let's dive a little deeper. Most of the time we have experience in buying products in the marketplace. For example, buying a car, buying groceries, buying a book etc. Those are all products, right? But hiring an immigration lawyer is actually buying knowledge, experience and service. There's a huge difference between the two.

Let me explain. We immigrants come to the U.S. from different parts of the world and the mindset we bring is "negotiating mindset" to always haggle the price down.

One example of this is. Let's say a woman went to a farmer's market, a market where they sell vegetables or produce. She will go to a vendor and she will ask. How much are your potatoes? And the vendor says, well, it's $2 a pound (for example). Then, she will say. Across the street or on the other side of the farmer's market, the person right there is selling these potatoes for $1.50 per pound. So can you beat his price and can you sell me these potatoes for $1 per pound?

These are the very old fashion tactics that many people use and I saw many people using the same tactics when hiring an immigration lawyer.

Hey, don't get me wrong if you are trying to save money. I get that or if you are tight on your family budget. I get it. I am all for "more bang for your buck". But these negotiation tactics can be counterproductive in the immigration world.

Here is why? When you are hiring an immigration lawyer. You are hiring his or her knowledge, experience and most, his service and not a product like a cellphone, car or a sack of potatoes.

Ask yourself, would you want to "cut yourself short" by negotiating immigration attorney fees on your own case? That would be like cutting your own future in America or the future of your family! Because your future and the future of your family depends on the outcome of your immigration case?

But let's not worry about the immigration lawyer here. Let's consider you and your future here for a moment. Do you want to treat a lawyer who can alter your future like a vendor selling potatoes at the farmer's market? The answer is NO! But many do! I know you wouldn't.

What I recommend is don't haggle with your immigration lawyer about the fee. Be nice to him or her. Be polite with them. Be respectful to them. Do what they ask you to do for your own good. A good cooperative attitude of yours with your immigration lawyer goes a long way.

I have seen many clients argue, get angry, price-haggling and even yell at their lawyers. It's not helpful to you and to your future in America.

After all, lawyers are humans. They are professionals. Most of them have been practicing law for many years. But ask yourself, what would you do if you were in their position? Would you like to deal with an angry, problematic, nerve wrecking client or one with a good attitude? It does matter! Trust me!

Ask questions? There is no harm in it. Lawyers don't bite. Find out what kind of a service you will be getting? That could be a major difference between the dollar amount and lawyer to another.

Ask yourself this question. Do you want to hire the cheapest lawyer in town? If yes, why? Why do you want to put your immigration case in the hands of the cheapest immigration lawyer in town? The outcome of your immigration case can have an impact on your future and your next generations.

How much is your life worth to you? Is your immigration case important to you? If your immigration case goes well, how will it impact your life? Do you want to negotiate the immigration attorney's fee like with the mindset of bargaining in the farmer's market with the vendor for a sack of potatoes?

If you get a green card (permanent resident card) do you think that you will get a better job, better opportunity? When you become a US citizen, will you get a better job, better business or an American dream life? If you like to see yourself achieve those goals—an American dream—do you think that'll be worth it for spending a good amount on a good immigration lawyer?

The answer is YES.

But I can understand why people negotiate the fee. Mostly, because their budget is tight. If so, be upfront about it. Tell the lawyer, they will listen. Come clean and let them know, this is what I was thinking.

Can you help me out and work with me in some kind of a way? Do you have a payment plan?

An immigration lawyer would be more receptive towards your straightforwardness than you try to cut corners with him or her and lose a great opportunity for having a great immigration lawyer working on your case. Don't let your ego or pride come in your way! You deserve much better than that!

In fact, honesty and straightforwardness should be your number one policy in the consultation with your lawyer. You should inform your immigration lawyer as fast as possible in an effective and polite way. Put everything on the table, even if you cannot afford them. Let them help you. I've seen in my career many immigration lawyers have a soft spot. Many go out of their way to help people. They can make plenty of money through plenty of people. For many immigration lawyers it would not hurt them if they take on a case where they don't make a fortune on one case.

So don't buy "a sack of potatoes" because you aren't. Don't have that mindset of buying a product. Have a mindset that you are buying a professional service, knowledge, and the competence of an immigration lawyer. By asking the right questions in a straightforward manner.

Question of Guarantee

Let's discuss a very common question of "guarantee" many people ask.

So many people ask this question to lawyers whether there are any guarantees!

The simple answer is "there are no guarantees".

The reason one individual asks this question is very psychological. They are at the decision making stage of the consultation. They are thinking if they spend so much money, will it be worth it for them to spend this much money? What would be the outcome? Would it be worth their while?

The harsh reality is that a lawyer and a medical doctor in the U.S. cannot give any guarantees. That's why many medical professionals have us sign a consent form as soon as we enter their office. So don't ask this question to a lawyer, save your time by asking other important questions. After all, you have limited time with the immigration lawyer during the consultation.

Don't believe me? Go ahead ask them!

Big tip! If an immigration lawyer gives you a guarantee . I would run far away from that lawyer. Because he or she cares about your wallet, not you. Such a lawyer wants your money. Most likely doesn't care about anything else.

The lawyer I used to work with used to answer this question sometimes like this. "If I can guarantee that you get a green card (permanent resident card) then I will charge you $200,000 for this case." Lol.

This is the harsh reality. Immigration lawyers cannot give guarantees. Because immigration lawyers are not the decision makers on your case. Immigration authorities are! So immigration lawyers cannot outright say they guarantee their immigration case.

Other Pointers for the Consultation You should Consider

"Everything of a significance will ALWAYS have an opposition, if not, it's not significant enough."

~ Nasir "Uncle Sammy" Qureshi

One time I was between the jobs and I was looking for any immigration paralegal job to support my family. So I went for an interview with an immigration lawyer and he hired me on the spot. But when I walked in his office, his office was messy.

There were papers and files everywhere. I mean everywhere. He even had files on the floor on the side of his office. The papers covered his entire desk like a table cloth included past bills, envelopes, mail, and office supply shattered all over the desk. There were stacks of clients' files on each side of his office desk and one side of the office floor.

When I arrived at his office, he tried to give me an impression with his office junk that he was a very busy lawyer.

Yes, that's true! Some lawyers keep all the files around their desk under the impression that it will show their clients that they are very busy.

But by working with him for a few weeks. I found out the opposite was true. He was not busy as he pretended with stacks of files and papers.

During my interview, he even cut his fingernails right in front of me while we were talking. (I am not joking).

As his paralegal for a very short period of time, I found out he was very unorganized. He did not have a good filing system. He looked for clients' files right in front of them.

I felt very uncomfortable. I turned in my resignation and found another law firm to work for. I was out of there!

So here are some pointers for you to consider. Please look out for these pointers while talking to an immigration lawyer:

-How much attention they are giving you in your presence?

-Are they listening to you?

-Is the lawyer making notes while you are talking to him or her?

(This could be a sign that they are paying attention to you)

-Are they answering your questions or concerns or doing the formality, nodding their heads and dodging your actual questions?

-Are they accepting calls during your consultation?

(If they are accepting calls, try to pay attention to what kind of call they are attending. A true emergency call from their family member or general calls from their existing clients that they can take after your consultation. If they are taking calls while you are there as they would anytime. That's not a good sign. Because they should respect your time. This means that they are not taking you seriously. Because your case is important to you so it should be to him or her. This could be a red flag and being unprofessional).

-Are they calling their staff, including other lawyers, paralegals or office secretaries and blaming them for not doing clients work right in front of you?

(Some lawyers do that after listening to the complaints of their angry clients to put their staff under the bus and to make an angry client happy).

-How clean is their office?

-How clean is their office desk?

-How organized is their office or their overall office space?

(If their office is not organized, guess what, how they would treat your file when you are not there? Just like the other files. Laying around everywhere. That's a red flag).

-How many staff members are working there as you can see while walking to the office?

(So you can get a general idea how big is the law firm)

-How does the lawyer sit on his or her chair during the consultation while listening to you? Is he or she leaning back or leaning forward while talking to you?

(When someone sits leaning forward in a business meeting. It means they are showing interest in what you are saying).

-What kind of decorations do they have in their office?

(This could give you a general idea about the lawyers' personality type. Likes, dislikes or family or spiritual background of the lawyer. But not conclusive)

-What is the condition of their office furniture?

(This could give you an idea of how much he or she cares about the look of his/her office. How much the lawyer has invested in it or not?

After all, a law office for an immigration lawyer should be a very important place for him or her. Because that's where they make their living? This should also give you an idea whether a lawyer cares or does not care about how they have their office is set up).

(Some of the pointers above are debatable. But these pointers can give you a general idea and will help. Trust me!)

A quick lawyer joke :)

No Good Question Goes Unbilled …

A man went to a lawyer and asked what his fee was. "$100 for three questions," answered the lawyer. "Isn't that a little steep?" said the man. "Yes," said the lawyer. "Now, what's your third question?"

Google, Research on the Internet and Reviews

As we live in the information age. Everyone likes to do research. But I want you to understand that doing research, especially legal research for immigration law, requires some qualifications and understanding of immigration law. See, the Internet is a very good tool. I love it. I use it on a daily basis. But to do immigration law research. It's not a good idea without having prior qualified expertise.

If doing immigration law research on the Internet was a good idea, then why would we have immigration lawyers to begin? If you don't believe me, go to any immigration court and spend some time there observing. You will find that even immigration judges are learning the immigration law. Lawyers on opposite sides debate. New immigration law policies and changes in the law happen often.

Immigration law is very comprehensive and very complicated. In fact, I remember one time I was with an attorney. I was in a federal court in Houston, Texas, and a federal judge was saying that immigration law is so complicated and changes so much that before he starts learning immigration law, he realizes that immigration law has changed again a great deal (jokingly said the federal judge). So I don't recommend you to "research" immigration law on the Internet. It would further confuse and stress you!

I would not recommend you to do a law research on the Internet for your immigration case. Leave that to the professionals who go to school and learn how to do that. What I do recommend is that you do your best to research a good immigration lawyer. How long has he or she been practicing immigration law? What do people say about this immigration lawyer? And once you find one, put everything on the table before the immigration lawyer. All the facts about your immigration case, background, and what would you like to see happen? What is your objective? Ask the right questions about your case and the lawyer. Then, whatever that lawyer tells you, don't second guess it or try to validate his or her professional opinion from your relatives, the Internet or another lawyer. Instead, run with his or her advice. Take action and change your life and move on with other things that are more important to you. Let your immigration lawyer worry about your immigration case. You are paying him or her to do exactly that.

Doing law research for your immigration case without having a qualified immigration law background or training adds more stress.

Here is why, first of all, Google is a search engine, not a research engine. Let alone not a "law search engine". It's a big difference.

In law, there are "law search engines" that are for the lawyers and paralegals. They are actually research engines that lawyers and law firms pay a price or subscriptions to use. For example, one of them is called Lexisnexis. And the second common one is WestLaw among the popular ones. They are quite expensive. But let's say if you have good law search experience or you are one of those types of people that you have to really look up information and are a fast learner, etc. Then, you can use another law search engine designed for legal professionals but is much more affordable called "Case Clerk " located at www.caseclerk.com. You will have access to a complete law library, infinite legal information and history of cases like any competent lawyer or law firm in the U.S. would.

The United States Citizenship & Immigration Services (USCIS) also has a great website with tons of great information about the immigration law www.uscis.gov. They constantly try to make it better.

But the main question is how does all that information apply to you? You need professional help to tell you what applies to you or not. And that is where immigration lawyer comes in to help you out.

Don't get me wrong, if you want to prepare your own case without the help of an immigration lawyer, by all means go for it. As public information, everyone knows that you have the legal rights to do so. In fact, this is a United States constitutional right, that you can represent yourself before any decision maker, adjudicator, court or any jurisdiction. But the question is do you want to risk your future? This book is not for people who want to represent themselves before any immigration authorities. In fact, this book is for the opposite group of the people, who want to be represented by an immigration lawyer. But needs a little coaching to find a good one.

Many people try to do their own case by themselves, not knowing what they are doing or taking a risk. If that's the case, please don't turn a good immigration case into a bad case by doing it yourself. I see that happens a lot. Why not do this thing right one time and get it over with and move on with your life?

One thing I would like you to understand that when we are filing any paperwork with the USCIS, United States citizenship and immigration services or with the US Department of Homeland Security, immigration court, or any federal agency or any court or with any decision maker in the United States of America. You are creating an administrative record.

Now, if you are doing it yourself and you make a mistake, guess what? That'll be a permanent mistake that you just made on a permanent record. If you make a mistake in your paperwork with immigration authorities, that's a hard thing to overcome, so why take a risk?

There are two fundamental reasons that I have observed why people do their immigration case themselves. One is money or their ego.

I highly recommend you don't do it yourself. If you're tight on money, find out how you can come up with money or find a lawyer and come clean to them that your budget is tight and if they can help you with the budget. Get a different job, drive Uber part time or borrow money, do whatever you can or take payment plans. Sometimes it's okay to be a little bit vulnerable and talk to a lawyer and I'm very low on money. How can you help me?

Do whatever you can! But my main concern is this: don't mess up your good immigration case just because it's out of your budget. If that's the case when you are short in money to hire a good hire immigration lawyer, then you have two problems. One immigration problem and the other a financial problem. But hiring a good immigration lawyer can help you solve both of those problems, should you be successful with the outcome of your immigration case with a good immigration lawyer's help.

Many people mess up their good case by doing it themselves. Then, they come to an immigration lawyer to do a cleanup job. Now the job for immigration lawyer handling your case is double the work; costing you more money. So let's not play as an "Attorney Google".

CHAPTER FOUR

"ATTORNEY GOOGLE"

"The Hispanic community understands the American dream and have not forgotten what they were promised- that in the U.S., a free market system, allow us all to succeed economically, achieve stability and security for your family and leave your children better off than yourselves."

~ United States Senator Marco Rubio

Second, I noticed that people go to immigration lawyers, seek consultation, whether they're free or paid consultations. They go and get some information from an immigration lawyer in consultation. Now they're going to Google that information, whether an immigration lawyer is saying the truth or not. My question to you, if you knew it, why did you go to immigration lawyer to begin with? That doesn't even make sense. The only reason people do that is because they have trust issues. This has nothing to do with the immigration lawyer but it has a lot to do with YOU.

You might have had some issues in the past at one time. Someone whether or not an immigration lawyer, or any lawyer from another area of law or any individual may have broken your trust or at least you thought they did. Well, if that is the case, I would like to remind you of an American old saying, "You can't change the past but you can definitely do something about your future".

Use this book as your guide and use common sense. Do whatever you can to find a good lawyer, trust him or her, meet your financial obligation with them, respect them, and run with the information they provide you and focus on other things in your life that are important to you and leave the rest to the higher power (If you believe in it) and your newly hired competent immigration lawyer. (Plus, it will keep your stress level down).

I am not sure why so many people spend so many hours, days and months just going from lawyer to lawyer thinking they are looking for a good immigration lawyer. Meanwhile, they are not even sure how to hire a good immigration lawyer? This method could be very tasking, stressful and very time consuming. You deserve better than this old fashioned uninformed hiring process for your next immigration lawyer.

Another mistake I see so many times is that people will go seek some consultation with an immigration lawyer, sit down with a lawyer for fifteen or twenty minutes and they get a little bit of information. Then they go see another lawyer for a consultation and they believe that they got enough information to do it themselves. They go file their own case. Please don't do that either.

There are other types of "Google immigration lawyers". People that have researched or "they look things up" on the internet because they think their case is very simple or they think they know what they are doing. Some people would think. My relatives, my cousin did it, my grandmother did it, my father did it, or they think they did it for many people and they became overconfident and do it themselves. Don't do this either.

But here is the problem with this scenario when some people file a case under the belief that they had enough knowledge to do so. Then, after a few months immigration sends them a notice, what we call it a Request for Evidence or a Request for Initial Evidence or any notice in which immigration asks for more information from them.

Now they don't know what to do. So now they go back to a lawyer or on Google looking for that information. Now they're playing "Attorney Google" or learning the immigration law through Google. If you are facing this situation, take my advice and do yourself a huge favor and just go hire you a good immigration lawyer to avoid all this. Because you can't afford to take such a risk.

This way you are letting a professional handle your immigration case. Your stress level would not be high. Meanwhile, you are focusing on other things in your life that are important to you besides your immigration case.

Side note.

I learned from many successful people the concept of delegating tasks to others and to professionals makes life more productive. That we should delegate tasks and assignments to others when we can. This saves us time to do other things.

This concept applies here most definitely.

Should You Look at the Reviews About an Immigration Lawyer?

We live in the age where we look at the reviews first before we buy things. I do too (you did the same thing before buying my book here, lol). But the question is should you look at the reviews of an immigration lawyer to weigh in your decision to hire him or her or not? How much should you weigh in this factor in your decision?

The answer is yes and no. Yes, you should consider reviewing the reviews on an immigration lawyer. But don't make your final decision based on this factor alone. People can be easily influenced by looking at the reviews on a website or elsewhere on the internet about an immigration lawyer.

I would recommend you look into the reviews of an immigration lawyer if you are planning to do so <u>BEFORE</u> meeting the lawyer and not after! Why, because if you have a concern about a review or two that you read about the lawyer. You would have an opportunity to bring it up with the lawyer during the consultation but not afterwards. So the lawyer can address it. (If a review is concerning you).

You wouldn't have the similar opportunity for the lawyer to address a bad review after you meet the lawyer. So it's a great idea to review the reviews for an immigration lawyer before meeting him or her not after.

How to Look at the Reviews?

When someone reads a review, first of all, you don't know that person who wrote the review about the immigration lawyer. More than likely you will never meet that person.

You'd most likely see reviews on an open platform on the Internet like Google, Google + pages, blogs etc. where there is no control or process of verification of an authentic or a verified review like www.amazon.com or www.thumbtack.com or www.thervo.com which has protocols to see if the reviews are authentic and verified or not. In fact, these sites have their own legal departments and teams that are working to make sure listed professionals and reviews are authentic, so consumers can have a good "real" experience as much as possible. Compared to finding reviews on any search engines anywhere about an immigration lawyer is not dependable.

I would recommend you not to give too much attention to any good or a bad review about an immigration lawyer or immigration law firm anywhere on Google, Google +, or Yelp pages because those reviews can be bought (good or bad).

Don't believe me? Check out www.fiverr.com and type "review" in the search box. Or Google this "companies to get reviews on google". There are big companies. That's all they do is help businesses get good reviews and eliminate bad ones.

There are also websites and companies that are in business on the Internet for the sole purpose of getting money from businesses to take off a negative review from their website when an angry individual places a negative review. For example, www.ripoffreport.com is a website that has a good search engine optimization team working for them. When an angry individual uses words such as "ripped off" or "complaint". This website pops up. Angry person writes a negative review and gets their chance to "vent out" a bit. Then business owners against whom the negative reviews were written start getting all sorts of emails from www.ripoffreport.com about how much they will charge to take that negative review off. Of course, the average person would NEVER see this side of the picture or this side of the coin what companies are really up to and why such a website exists to begin with.

(Just a tip—if you think an immigration lawyer has ripped you off. Then writing a negative review on the web anywhere will not get your hard earned money back. Neither state bar where the lawyer is licensed from has any jurisdiction (authority) to get you your money back.) You may want to file a lawsuit to do that in the justice of peace court or any other civil court where it is the proper jurisdiction and you need to consult with an attorney for that.

Let's say, if a person has allegedly had a bad experience with an immigration lawyer and he wrote a bad review about an immigration lawyer or for the law firm. You also want to look at the response of that immigration lawyer or law firm about that review. (If any are available.)

If you see a negative review about an immigration lawyer or an immigration law firm that you are considering to hire, look at how many are good reviews and how many are bad? If a lawyer has more bad reviews than good reviews, then it's a no brainer not to waste your time even scheduling consultation with his or her office. But if the lawyer has more good reviews and few bad reviews, then this is normal. Even I have bad reviews. Everyone does!

A quick lawyer joke :)

Take the Bad with the Badder ...

What's the difference between a good lawyer and a bad lawyer? A bad lawyer might let a case drag on for several years. A good lawyer knows how to make it last even longer.

Contents of a Review!

Please pay attention to the contents of the review! This is very important. Many people don't! It's a big mistake. What do I mean by the contents of the review?

Let me explain. You should find out what the review is actually saying. Is the review about the immigration lawyer himself or herself? Is the review about the staff of the law firm? Is the review about not being able to return calls enough? Is the review about the lack of knowledge of an immigration lawyer? Is a review about a client not getting the result they were expecting? Or a negative review about "taking money" from clients and not doing anything. (A very common negative review.) All those things are very subjective. The different reviews do really matter.

For example, if a bad review is about the staff and not the lawyer themselves. This is not a big deal because in many immigration law firms, staff like the front desk receptionist frequently changes. If someone wrote a review a few years ago about their bad experience with a front desk receptionist, well, there are great chances that a particular front desk secretary may not still be working there. And if she is, she's not going to work on your immigration case, should you decide to hire that immigration lawyer. An immigration lawyer or a legal assistant would.

I don't want to analyze all the common bad reviews here. But I do want to bring in your attention to consider a common sense factor that if a person wrote a negative review about an immigration lawyer is not a lawyer to begin with and has LIMITED knowledge of immigration law. Should we even consider that review? Is the written review about the service of the lawyer or the knowledge of the lawyer or the immigration law itself? That's why it is very important to pay close attention to the content of a good or bad written review.

I recommend that you don't get too hung up on the reviews in making your final decision about hiring an immigration lawyer.

CHAPTER FIVE

HOW DO IMMIGRATION LAWYERS CHARGE?

I heard a lawyer joke once is worth mentioning here.

"A 50-year-old lawyer who had been practicing since he was 25 passed away and arrived at the Pearly Gates for judgment. The lawyer said to St. Peter, "There must be some mistake! I'm only 50 years old, that's far too young to die." St. Peter frowned and consulted his book. "That's funny, when we add up your billing records, you should be at least 83 by now!" ~ Anonymous

The most important factor in any business transaction is the "money". Nothing else is more important to most people when it comes to making a decision. Whether it is buying a car, clothes, house, groceries, cell phone, even getting a job, opening a business, hiring a lawyer is not any different!

Many people who are in the market for hiring an immigration lawyer keep this "money factor" up front when making a decision which lawyer to hire or not.

Some of the factors in the decision making process were discussed in this book already. But let's look at how immigration law firms charge their clients. This can also help you in making a good decision on "how to hire an immigration lawyer?" or which one?

There are three different ways immigration lawyer and immigration law firms charge their clients:

1. Partial fee and partial upon completion;

2. Detailed billing; and

3. Flat fee

1. Partial Fee and Partial Upon Completion:

In practical terms, let's say you made your initial payment to start your immigration case out of $4,000. (total amount.) The lawyer may ask you to pay $1,000 out of that to start working on your immigration case or $2,000. But will ask you for the remainder of the fee right before he or she shows up for your interview or last hearing on your case. The reason an immigration lawyer does that is to make sure you pay fully what you both agreed upon. Sometimes clients disappear after the last hearing or their interview with the USCIS and keep the lawyer hanging, if they did not complete paying their lawyer. Yes, that's true. Some people don't care!

In this type of billing, the client actually knows the full amount of money an immigration lawyer would be charging to represent them. Good thing about this billing is that the client has a certainty factor of the total charge. They know the total amount of immigration attorney's fee. There are no uncertainties about how much it would actually cost them as it is in the "Detailed billing".

2. Detailed billing:

Another way some immigration lawyers charge their clients is called "detailed billing" where clients charge a client in increments as the case progresses. Clients deposit some money with the lawyer like filling gasoline in your car and the car will run. No gas in the car. Car does not run!

In this case, a detailed billing is called invoice billing as well, where a lawyer articulates every single charge and expense and invoices their clients.

For example, if a lawyer sends out a certified mail letter in their case, they will indicate that in the next invoice and charge it accordingly to their clients.

If there is a paralegal that charges $30 working on your case at the law firm, they will show how many hours the paralegal worked on your case in the last month and how much of that money you paid last month was used accordingly. This type of billing can include anything and everything that you know and don't know being used or a lawyer utilized working on your immigration case or in support of your case.

Positive factor of this type of billing from the client's perspective is that you know exactly how your money has been spent. Sometimes down payment or "the start up fee" is low (or sometimes it appears low). You can get started working with an immigration lawyer.

The downside of this type of billing from a client's perspective is that you will never know how much it will cost you as a total amount when immigration lawyer is done.

Tell you the truth! Many lawyers end up making all sorts of things, charges and billable hours for themselves and for their staff in such invoices to clients. There is no way for you to confirm or dispute that since the lawyer is the one in charge of your case.

3. Flat Fee

Another way and the most common way immigration lawyers charge their clients is called "the flat fee". Most of the immigration law firms go with flat rate billing during the consultation. In this scenario, you and your immigration lawyer will discuss how much they will charge in representing your immigration. For example, let's say if you're filing for your spouse who is an immigrant and you are a U.S. citizen. You're filing a green card application or and a permanent residence status for your spouse. For example, in the flat fee agreement, your attorney will charge you $2,500 flat rate to do the whole job up to the interview of what we call it, a green card interview or the interview for permanent residency.

In this option, attorney's fees, expenses, paralegal fees and filling out the applications everything will cover that except the government fees. Some people charge government fees also in the flat fee, but most immigration lawyers don't. They specify and exclude it.

When the attorney's fees or the charges are discussed, you may want to also ask these questions.

Does this include the filing fees?

Filing fee is the government fees that are required for immigration forms, applications and motions before the immigration courts are required to pay along with your paperwork.

You should ask the immigration lawyer:

Does it exclude the government filing fee or does the total quote include the government's filing fee?

You can also ask your immigration lawyer:

What is included in the attorney's fees?

You may also want to ask this question:

If it's going to be any appeal, then will it be a different charge for that?

Most of the immigration lawyers charge separate attorney's fees for filing an appeal because filing an appeal is a separate case at the separate jurisdiction. (before the separate decision makers).

(Note: despite what type of billing or a method your immigration lawyer charges his or her clients. Most of the immigration lawyers EXCLUDE the government filing fee in their quotes. But they do inform you about them in advance).

Some law firms just charge one amount to respond to the Requests for Evidence, which is given by immigration because they need some information from you and they will not make a decision until they receive this case or one fee to file a legal instrument or a legal document (like a motion in an immigration court).

Thus, it's a good question that you want to ask a law firm or lawyer during the consultation, what is included in the attorney's fees?

At the conclusion, I would recommend you have the lawyer write the terms and fee agreement in a contract or some call it "retainer agreement". Most lawyers do that but unfortunately, I have seen many lawyers don't write a contract.

It's absolutely fine with you not to rush reading a contract and asking questions about it with your lawyer. Then sign it once you are comfortable.

Interview of Ivan Sanchez

Who is Ivan Sacnhez?

Ivan Sanchez emigrated from Colombia at his young age to the United States. He currently lives in Houston, Texas. He worked as a senior congressional liaison, a head of an immigration department for a United States Congresswoman Sheila Jackson Lee's office. He has served on the Houston's Mayor Advisory Board and was the founder of Houston's Millennials Non-Profit Organization. He has a degree in Political Science from University of Houston-Downtown. He is a vocal community activist and often speaks for the rights of the immigrant community.

At his job, Ivan communicated with the federal agencies such as USCIS, ICE, DHS, and FBI to inquire about immigration cases on a daily basis. He is well aware of challenges in the immigrant community and the world of immigration lawyers. He brings a great insight to this topic.

(Exact Interview)

Nasir: How are you Ivan?

Ivan: Let me begin by saying happy Halloween to whoever celebrates it out there and thank you for taking your time to write such an important book. Such a vital book for our immigrant community. Let me fix something for your introduction. I'm a former congressional candidate, and I am a dreamer with papers. Sometimes I don't know how lucky I am to have that piece of paper. But there is absolutely no difference between myself and a dreamer. The only difference is that I have a piece of paper that is all I was brought here through no fault of my own.

I am educated. I put myself through college. So there is no distinction between a dreamer and myself, right? So, yes, I'm an immigrant from Colombia. My parents brought me when I was six years old, at no fault of my own here. It was just my mother with three kids, and like any other immigrants. We are the new blood that's inserted into the countries. We are not here to take jobs. Actually, my mother created more than a thousand jobs when she was alive. Now my two other brothers have two separate companies employing more than 500 people between each other. So they wouldn't take anybody's job. No. And, but that's their profession. But for me, what did I do after school? I started working in the United States Congress, but just because I had that piece of paper, I was able to help hundreds of immigrants get their benefits. Also, I was able to help hundreds of people out of wrongful deportations.

So yes, I did run for Congress. Unfortunately, I fell behind, but that's okay. I'm a 30-year-old, a Hispanic activist, not only Hispanic activist, but a community activist. So I look forward to the future and your questions about immigration.

Nasir: Thank you so much for what you do, sir. Would you consider yourself also as an immigration social activist?

Ivan: I mean, that's what I meant as a Hispanic advocate. I mean, I worked as an immigration liaison in the United States Congress for five years. I worked with the Department of Defense with Immigration & Customs Enforcement (ICE), Federal Bureau of Investigation (FBI), the State Department, the International Council across the world to help people get their visas, to stop these deportations, to get people their green cards (permanent resident cards), employment authorization documents and help people get their U.S. citizenship etc.

So with so many different things. I'm very interested in the topic of how we're going to go to this million dollar question now. How to find the right immigration lawyer?

Just because you are an immigration attorney does not mean that you are, that person, man or woman is going to fix your issue. This is not the case. I've had cases when I worked in the United States Congress and if they call Congress and you know, a lot of Hispanics don't or a lot of minorities don't. We don't even know what Congress is. But when they call congress it is such an urgent matter that they have to call somebody. I will pick up these phone calls and I found out that the entire situation was created by their immigration attorneys. Especially here in the city of Houston. We have factories of immigration attorneys now that they just pipeline people, take people's money knowing that they're going to lose.

And that is happening nationwide not only in Houston, Texas alone. I can call so many immigration lawyers by names who do that. But I won't right now.

The problem is not only bad immigration attorneys. But also many organizations who claim to help immigrants, but they're charging a whopping fee. Then, they tell the immigrant to get out of my office, or I'll call ICE on you. This is what's happening in the everyday community. But because the immigrant community is such an unempowered community. We're empowering in what we can bring to the community. But unempowered yet because we still are fighting

68

for their status or our status or what not. But I hope that through this discussion you guys will learn a bit or two on how to shop for the right immigration attorney.

Nasir: Thank you, Mr. Ivan, you bring a very important, unique experience to this book and to our society. Because one you are an immigrant yourself. As you mentioned, you also work for a United States Congress, as a liaison, heading the immigration department and work with several, several nonprofit organizations and you also know what's going on nationwide.

So, what advice would you give to an immigrant that he or she actually wants to fix their papers or status in the U.S.?

Ivan: That's a perfect question. Beautiful question. A complex question because the thing is that you and I are privileged. We have the knowledge, we have connections, we have everything when we're talking about this issue. We should do it with sympathy and understanding and put ourselves in the shoes of the immigrants. When you migrated, imagine the issue that you had. Language barriers, financial difficulties, lack of social circles. It goes on and on, right? What I would say, so the people that come to our congressional office, I couldn't refer them to a specific attorney that will be a conflict of interest. But I would say go to AILA (American Immigration Lawyers Association) www.aila.org It is like an eBay of lawyers.

You can filter them by what their concentration of law practice is? You don't want to hire a deportation lawyer to fix your visa or you don't want to hire a visa lawyer to do your deportation case. It's totally different. It's one industry of immigration law. But everything doesn't work under the same thing. So you can see their ratings. They're one with bad reviews,and good reviews or both.

But the issue here is deeper. Because the typical immigrant or a Hispanic immigrant wouldn't know how to navigate social media, websites, or the web in general as much. So it's not as easy as telling them go, read, go to www.aila.org and shop around, right?

So this is a big issue. But somehow we have to solve this bigger issue through books like this.

I hope that this information filters through the right channels, and people's lives. Because there are serious consequences in the future for the future of the immigrants because their lives are at stake. So one of the things I would say is find, let's say if they do go to AILA or they have a friend that's helping the friend personally look for this specialty that they need. Again, if they need a green card, please do not go to an attorney that is doing a car accident or corporate law or please do not go to a place where they're charging $300 bucks for a consultation or $300 bucks for the entire thing. And if there's a line outside of immigrants waiting like some of these immigration factories, many immigration lawyers are running, most definitely, you don't want to go there.

You want to go somewhere where they specialize or primarily focus in immigration law. Are they going to sit with you or not? Are they going to answer all your questions or not? Because what you are doing as an immigrant, as a future American citizen, you're shopping around and that person (the immigration lawyer) that you're hiring is going to work for you. So if they're too busy, if they think they're too cool or too important? Walk away! There are many, many attorneys.

But again, there are so many of these immigration lawyers factories. That it's sad. You could have the best product in the world, but if nobody knows about it, it's worthless.

What do some of these immigration lawyer factories do? They go to every single Hispanic radio station and act like they're our savior and pronounce themselves and introduce themselves like there's no other attorney but them. But you do not need to be fooled by these commercials. I urge immigrants to do your research. It is a life or death situation at the end of the day!

Nasir: Mr. Ivan, would you agree with me that hiring the right help, hiring a right immigration attorney or just any immigration attorney or not a good immigration attorney could be a difference between achieving the American dream or deportation?

Ivan: Like I said, working in the congressional office I would quickly find out by looking at alot cases that why the heck did this immigration attorney turn in this form?

There is no way to do it, and these immigration attorneys are putting these immigrants in such an awkward position that they literally end up in deportation proceedings because of their own immigration attorney. So look around, do your homework and hire a good immigration lawyer for your case.

Don't be afraid to call immigration lawyers. Call them and ask how their process is. How much do they charge for a consultation fee? How much are their services? How much are the forms? Because the forms are actually free. If someone's charging you for a form, tell them. Bye. It's the most illegal thing to do is to sell immigration forms. But some lawyers actually even do that, and they get away with it. Because what an immigrant is going to do? Are they going to hire another attorney to sue the attorney? No, they trust in this man and believe in him "this person in a suit, man or woman, whatever. But yes, it's a life and death situation, no doubt!

Nasir: Does an immigrant who's going through the immigration process has some kind of a way for voicing themselves before the congressional offices?

Ivan: Yes, one hundred percent problem is getting information to the immigrant. And the second problem would be how? Imagine how scared an immigrant would be to contact a member of Congress to have the courage enough to do so. Yeah. Sometimes they're up against a wall. But sometimes their friends, teachers, or their family members that actually made contact with Congressional offices or something like that. But our government is separated into three branches: legislative, executive, and judicial. The legislative is divided into two. The United States Senate and The United States House of the Representatives (U.S. Congress). They are voted to represent a certain constituency. For example, senators who represent the entire state. Congressional representatives only represent a certain section of your state.

But in Congress, if you live in a district, you will serve as a constituent, you are like a boss of the representative. You can call and say I need a meeting with your immigratio liaison like I was. I met with thousands of people, and if they charge, you will let the author of the book or myself know and we'll sue them. We'll sue the entire office. They aren't supposed to charge anything. But what they do is push for your case inside the government. It's a service you voted for that member of Congress. Maybe you didn't vote for them because you couldn't vote as an immigrant. But still, that representative represents you. I mean, it makes sense to call the office and ask for immigration liaison and tell them your problem and what they do is that they're not your attorney. But they will contact the director of immigration or deputy director of Immigration or the field office and say, put your case in front of them saying. Look at this case, I believe it needs reconsideration or a closer look or whatever it is and get some answers. You have no idea how many attorneys would call me for help.

There's hundreds and thousands of immigration attorneys, but only a few immigration liaisons.

You need to use what you have, right? You need your papers, or you need permission to leave the country or your status. And your attorney is saying, 30 more days, 30 days, 30 more days? It might be true or might not be.

But you can call your member of Congress, talk to the immigration liaison and ask for an expedite request. I just did it in a meeting before this one. A young lady was going to get married. She's an immigrant, but she's an attorney from Mexico and in Mexico. But she's here. She was here on a business visa but needed to get married. She was getting married in Mexico. But she couldn't leave the United States, so she asked for that permission to leave and it was taking long until she contacted me. I got it through. It was expedited, and now she's happily married. So use your resources.

Nasir: Fantastic, what one advice would you give to immigrants who come to the United States?

Ivan: Stay out of trouble and stay out of trouble! Don't drink and drive. Don't get drunk in public places. I don't know where some immigrants come from but do not touch your wife. Do not hit your kids, don't break the law and everything will be fine.

Nasir: Thank you so much, Mr. Ivan, for what you do. I really appreciate your time. Thank you.

Ivan: No thank you for what you are doing by writing this book. Such a book is truly needed. It will be a great help!

(End of the interview)

CONCLUSION

I hope that you have enjoyed this book and got a good idea for how to hire an immigration lawyer? I tried my best to leave the fluff out of this book. I kept myself to the point, legal language (legalese) to the minimum so an average person without any prior background of law can understand this book easily.

Also, I did my best to give you public information and provided an inside window into the world of immigration lawyers, what really happens "behind the scenes".

Now, when you hear "consult with an immigration lawyer for legal advice".

Now you know, which one! (or how to find one)

Pretty please! *(like my children say at home)* :)

Please do me a HUGE personal favor, leave a review on Amazon. If you like this book, please recommend this book to others so others may also benefit from it.

Best wishes,

Nasir "Uncle Sammy" Qureshi

Nasir Qureshi

Houston, Texas

www.nasirqureshi.com

nasirqureshiauthor@gmail.com

ABOUT THE AUTHOR

Nasir "Uncle Sammy" Qureshi lives in Houston, Texas with his wife and three children. Author is an immigrant and came to the U.S at a young age. Today, he responsibly cares for the special needs of his family and enjoys doing home-based online business, mentoring and leading many around the world.

Among many other career accomplishments, Nasir spearheaded the growth of a Houston-based immigration law firm to be ranked #1 immigration law firm in Texas for 2014-2016 on the internet. He retired from a 12-year of a fulfilling career as a senior immigration paralegal in 2019.

Author is a former Houston Newspaper Columnist. He speaks nine different languages and enjoys doing personal development to stretch his mind and his education. He has built a habit of reading books of personal development, business, and spiritual growth resulting in reading over 1300 books since 1997 (minimum one book a week). Author often quotes *"The more I learn, the more I know how much I don't know"*. So the author's journey of learning and teaching others continues.

Author believes in:

"Personal Development before Fortune." ~ Jim Rohn

"Ask not what your country can do for you - ask what you can do for your country." ~ John F. Kennedy

"You can have everything in life you want, if you just help other people get what they want." ~ Zig Ziglar

A THANK YOU NOTE!

Quick question.

You get a cellphone or a utility bill?

Would it be ok if it's less or even free?

Yes, free. I am not joking. Out of my appreciation for buying this book and reading it so far. I want to thank you and show my appreciation.

Visit my other website. https://www.nasirqureshi.com/bills-crusher/

Watch a one minute video and complete the contact form. My team will contact you and help you get qualified for a free cell   phone service. So you can save some money every month and spend that money on anything you like but a cellphone.

This is part of my home-based business and what I do. When someone becomes a customer of any essential service and pays a bill. Portion of that is donated to feed a child in need through Feeding America, a non-profit charitable organization.